UPPER RHYMNEY VALLEY

THROUGH TIME

Ewart Smith

AMBERLEY PUBLISHING

Parc Cwm Darran
This sign welcomes you at the entrance to Cwm Darran Park, just above Deri. Vegetation over millennia was converted into coal and that coal was mined to provide our energy. Times have changed dramatically and, as this carving shows, an area that produced millions of tons of coal has been returned to nature.

This book is dedicated to my wife Betty in grateful recognition of all her help and assistance.

First published 2010

Amberley Publishing
Cirencester Road, Chalford,
Stroud, Gloucestershire, GL6 8PE

www.amberley-books.com

Copyright © Ewart Smith, 2010

The right of Ewart Smith to be identified as the
Author of this work has been asserted in accordance
with the Copyrights, Designs and Patents Act 1988.

ISBN 978 1 84868 742 4

British Library Cataloguing in Publication Data.
A catalogue record for this book is available from
the British Library.

Typeset in 9.5pt on 12pt Celeste.
Typesetting by Amberley Publishing.
Printed in the UK.

Introduction

As I have never lived in the Rhymney Valley, I feel I should offer some explanation as to why I agreed to write a book about it. My maternal grandmother lived in Gilfach, Bargoed, and we visited her frequently; I attended Lewis School, Pengam for eight years, so made many friends in the valley, with some of whom I am still in close contact; my wife spent her first twenty years in New Tredegar and a part of her adult life, before we married in Hengoed; my father-in-law was the senior partner in John Price & Sons, who had drapery shops in Rhymney, Pontlottyn, and New Tredegar (in fact, the Pontlottyn shop was where David Morgan traded before his department store opened in Cardiff). In addition, I have collected old postcards for decades. Most of them were of people and places in the Sirhowy Valley, but frequently I came across cards of other places I was familiar with, outside the Sirhowy Valley. I bought them for I could not leave a card at a postcard fair if I felt I had some association with it. All this meant that, before the project was even initiated, I had a great deal of the material in this book prepared. Friends and their contacts provided everything else.

What has changed during the period for which we have photographic evidence? Almost everything. The collieries of Ogilvie, Groesfaen, Bargoed, Elliot New Tredegar, Britannia, and Penallta have all disappeared. They employed many thousands of miners, but they are no more. The land on which they stood has been cleared and turned into parks. What used to be places of work have become places for leisure. Some even have small stretches of water populated by wildfowl.

A walk around any village in the valley, or indeed in any of the South Wales valleys, presents a similar scene. Many shops are boarded up or have been converted into houses and most of the chapels are closed. The open spaces where children used to play have been built on. There are cars and wheelie bins everywhere. In the larger towns, instead of shops selling food and household goods, there are travel agents, building societies, estate agents, and charity shops. To buy food, one must visit a supermarket. On a sadder note, the community spirit is not as strong as it used to be. There are not the choirs or dramatic, operatic, and musical societies; churches, chapels, and clubs do not organise trips to Barry or Porthcawl any longer; the local cinema has closed so we watch films in private. No longer can you have a smooth ride in a car. At some stage you will be forced to travel over strategically placed bumps in the road, placed there to reduce the speed of overenthusiastic young drivers. Another great loss is the demise of the Miners' Institutes. Almost every town and village had one. The 'stute had a library, a reading room, a concert or dance hall, and a billiard hall, later to be known as a snooker hall.

However, we all appreciate how much better life is for most of us today. Think of the benefits of electricity: heat and light, electric irons, washing machines and driers, refrigerators and deep freezers, radios and television sets. We have mobile phones. It is easy to travel vast distances. Our fathers and sons do not have to dig for coal in the bowels of the earth. Children are in full-time education until they are sixteen and have the opportunity to continue well beyond this age, a high percentage going on to gain degrees. We are better clothed and fed than we have ever been – perhaps too well fed. People are in better health and are living longer thanks to modern medicine and a National Health Service paid for with our taxes. Many simple changes are easy to forget – central heating rather than attending to coal fires, heating in the bedroom, insulation, hot water on tap, indoor toilets.

Outside, the roads and pavements are all surfaced so that we do not need to clean our footwear before going indoors, something that would have been unheard of a century ago. Electric street lighting is much better than gas lamps and is on throughout the night; our household waste is collected more hygienically; anything that can be recycled, is. It may be human nature to complain, but turning these pages you appreciate how, on the whole, things have dramatically improved over the period covered by these photographs.

Carno Cottages, Rhymney

One of the Carno Cottages near the entrance to Rhymney Cemetery and its chapel. Originally farm dwellings, with the animals and family under one roof, they were built of local sandstone and thatched with rushes. Later families would extract coal from the seams around them. In the scene today, improvements to this property are still ongoing.

Redwood Hospital
Opened in 1904 as Rhymney Cottage Hospital, this hospital was sponsored and maintained almost totally by The Rhymney Workmen's Medical Aid Fund; at one time, workmen paid 6*d* a week. Its name was changed to the Redwood Memorial Hospital in 1947 in recognition of Dr de Acton Redwood, who had served the hospital for forty-three years. Now belonging to the NHS, the building is still used for healthcare.

Rhymney Choirs

Under the baton of Daniel Owen, Rhymney Royal Male Voice Choir sang for Edward VII at Buckingham Palace in 1908. At this time, there were many choirs in and around the town: male voice, ladies', and mixed. Competition was fierce, often causing family friction. The modern photograph shows members of Rhymney Silurian Singers with their conductor Ralph Williams and accompanist Ashleigh Powell. Ralph has been associated with the choir for over forty-five years, leading them to the top award at the National Eisteddfod in Newport in 1988.

St. David's Church, Rhymney

Built of Pennant Sandstone by Rhymney Iron Company in the Doric style, St David's Parish Church was opened in 1843. Its glory is the stained glass window created by William Wailes *c.* 1856, which depicts the Ascension. The church is unusual for a parish church; the chancel is extremely short and there is a large balcony supported by unfluted columns. If anything, it looks more like a Nonconformist chapel than a parish church. Major restoration is taking place at the time of writing.

Pontlottyn Viaduct

This is a most unusual scene. It shows the Railway Inn, built in 1867 under two of the arches of Pontlottyn viaduct, on land rented from the railway company and erected against the wishes of the Rhymney Iron Company. In 1997, the railway company forced the removal of the inn with the pretext that they needed access to the underside of the arches for maintenance. Today there is a completely new road layout in the square, but trains still traverse the viaduct.

David Morgan's Early Shop, Pontlottyn

This property on The Square is where David Morgan, the founder of the well-known Cardiff department store, opened a drapery shop in 1858, just eight months after he had opened his first shop in Cwm Shon Matthew Square, Rhymney. When David Morgan left to open in Cardiff in 1879, he left his cousin John Price in charge. John eventually bought the business from his cousin; he and his sons continued in business here until the 1980s, when Cal White took it over.

The Square, Pontlottyn

Taken from the viaduct, this picture shows a Sunday school march through the village early in the nineteenth century. Smart clothes and headgear – particularly for the ladies – was the order of the day. The buildings on the left of The Square remain, but those to the right were removed some years ago for the widening of the road. The traffic between Pontlottyn and Rhymney now uses two of the viaduct's arches.

Board Street, Pontlottyn
This was on the opposite side of the viaduct to The Square. Its houses date back to the early part of the nineteenth century. The whole area was cleared to be replaced by new properties and green open spaces.

Pontlottyn Station

Notice the huge tips of industrial waste in the background. The substantial stone station building has been replaced by an open shelter. It is unmanned and the line is now a single track. The coal-fired steam train has been replaced by a modern diesel, which still provides a regular service between Rhymney and Cardiff.

Waterloo Terrace, Pontlottyn

Pontlottyn War Memorial was originally erected in the fork between Fochriw Road and Waterloo Terrace, but it is now on a secluded site off Chapel Street. When the junction was blocked off, traffic from Fochriw was rerouted to join the main road a little closer to the centre of the village, at a point that gives drivers much better visibility.

South End Terrace, Pontlottyn
The terrace is on the main road out of the village towards New Tredegar. The school crossing lady stands at the end of Greenfield Street. She is opposite the old vicarage, now Valley Manor Nursing Home.

Carnival Time in Fochriw

The beautifully turned-out Mini Paraders jazz band leads a procession of floats along Pontlottyn Road. Since then, much of the landscape has changed. The vast spoil tips in the background have been removed and a new leisure centre has been built just off camera, to the right.

Railway Terrace, Fochriw

The hill to the left led to Fochriw Colliery and the mountain roads that connect Gelligaer and Deri with the heads of the valleys. The building that remains, now a private house, was built in 1863 as a school. It was soon too small, so a new school was built next door. Over time, this school became the Co-operative Store and the 1863 building a Methodist Chapel. Behind the camera was The Rising Sun, a public house, now closed.

The Top of James Street, New Tredegar

Here we see the low railway bridge at the top of the street, with the English Congregational Church behind. There was also a Welsh Congregational Church nearby on the left. The railway line carried mineral traffic from the McLaren Colliery at Abertysswg, until the landslip between the two villages broke this link. Passenger traffic went as far as White Rose Station, which was just under the bridge to the left.

James Street from the River Bridge

Once this was a busy shopping street, with Barclays Bank on one side, John Price & Sons and Aaron Francis the chemist (later Boots) on the other. Every village sported a large hotel. In New Tredegar, it was the Tredegar Arms on the corner of Commercial Street and James Street. You wonder who filled these large hotels day after day. It was certainly not the miners.

Gas Street, New Tredegar
The old postcard I have names this Gas Street; modern street atlases show it as Sunnybank. It is on the western side of the river and opposite the old Town School. An expensive but necessary bridge has recently replaced the old one.

St. Dingat's, New Tredegar

St. Dingat's, the parish church at New Tredegar, was built in Pennant Sandstone by Seddon and Carter in 1892/3 with a chancel, a nave, and one aisle. The south aisle was added in 1899. The present scene shows an unusually ambitious war memorial, comprising two soldiers; one on alert, the other collapsing.

Looking East from Tirphil
The centre of New Tredegar, from a point south of the station on the lower road through Tirphil. The village of Phillipstown is on the horizon. Tirphil Station, which is still in use, is on the line connecting Rhymney and Cardiff.

The Tredegar Arms Hotel

This view of Tirphil from James Street, New Tredegar, could well have inspired the artist Lowry to paint one of his pictures of the valley. Many of these houses have been demolished. The parish hall has yet to be built, but the biggest change is the number of people on the street. On the right is the Italianate Tredegar Arms Hotel, with its cast-iron porch and relief lettering. It is thought to have been built more than 140 years ago.

The Town School, New Tredegar
This is near the river and opposite Gas Street (also known as Sunnybank). No longer a school, the building was converted into residential accommodation.

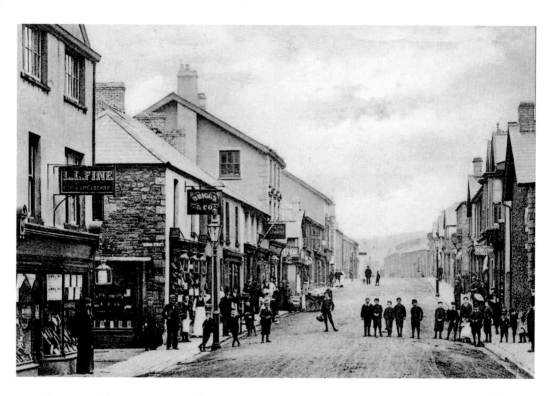

Commercial Street, New Tredegar

The view from James Street. Once a busy shopping street, it is now mostly populated by cars and wheelie bins.

Duffryn Street, New Tredegar

In the early part of the last century, our last ride would have been on the shoulders of bearers or in a horse-drawn hearse. The chief mourners would ride in a horse-drawn carriage while other mourners walked behind. Today, no one walks. Below are Anthony and Edward Williams-Price, directors of Stanley J. Nicholas, the only privately owned undertaking firm in the valley. Their Mercedes Benz Elegance hearse was the only one built by Pollmann of Bremen for the UK.

Elliot Colliery, New Tredegar

Sunk in 1888, Elliot Colliery produced more than a million tons of coal a year during the first decade of the last century. It was a very wet pit; eight tons of water were pumped away for every ton of coal raised. In 1912, the colliery was employing more than 2,800 miners. The colliery closed in 1967 when it was still producing more than half a million tons a year. The building to the left of the tower known now as the Winding House, survives.

Strawberry Valley

A row of houses overlooks the railway line at Strawberry Valley, better known as Cwmsyfiog, just south of New Tredegar. The houses and railway have long since gone, but several of the properties in the background are still identifiable. A new road now brings you directly into the centre of New Tredegar.

Ogilvie Colliery

Powell Duffryn's Ogilvie Colliery, just north of Deri, was opened in 1916 and was the company's last deep mine. It had been under pressure to close since 1969; a fire in 1971 closed one face and this accelerated the closure of the mine in 1975. The BBC filmed *Above Us the Earth* and a *Doctor Who* story, 'The Green Death', here. The area, now known as Parc Cwm Darran, has caravanning and camping facilities and a visitor centre.

Darran and Deri Station

The building on the left, now a house, is the only indication that we are in the same place. The railway was the artery into the Darran Valley from the Rhymney Valley and was essential to the transportation of coal from the Ogilvie and Groesfaen pits to the ports at Newport and Cardiff. The former railway line is now part of a surfaced path, which encourages rural walks. There is the occasional bench, where one can sit and contemplate the world.

Deri Post Office
This is a lovely old photograph of Deri Post Office and a branch of the New Tredegar & District Co-operative Society. These, and the other two shops, supplied most of the immediate needs of the village. Unlike today, everybody wanted to be photographed.

Groesfaen Colliery

This colliery was sunk in 1902-06 by the Rhymney Iron Company. At 2,160 feet, it was the deepest colliery in the Darran Valley, whose waters, known as Nant Bargod Rhymni, flow into the Rhymney River at Bargoed. Production began in 1908 and ceased in 1969. It employed around 700 miners. Today, it is difficult to believe that there was ever a colliery on this spot. The site has become a public park.

The Church Inn, Bedwellty

Local riders assemble with their hounds on a rather muddy unmade road outside the Church Inn in the early part of the last century. The walls on the right form part of the church's boundary wall. A large water butt and two short pipes illustrate how important it was to preserve the available water – there was no piped water. Today, the spruced-up inn, until recently with a greyhound racing track adjacent, still thrives.

St Sannan's Church, Bedwellty (I)

High on the ridge, claiming to belong to both valleys (Rhymney and Sirhowy) is the ancient church of St Sannan's. Sannan was an Irish contemporary of St David. The present building dates from *c.* 1220, but it was extended, and a tower was added, in the fourteenth century. A vestry was added when major restoration took place at the beginning of the last century. A further restoration at the beginning of this century resulted in a new roof and the whole building being whitewashed.

Interior, Bedwellty Church, near Aberbargoed.

St. Sannan's Church, Bedwellty (II)

Part of the chancel, viewed from the south aisle. Pews at the rear of the church have been removed to allow better use of space. The chancel contains the treasure of the church, an old vestment chest dating from *c.* 1450. The side-on view to the congregation exhibits two panels; the upper one depicts pierced hands, a heart, and feet, surrounded by a crown of thorns, the lower one a shield with three nails, a scourge, a hammer, and a spear.

The Neuadd Wen, Aberbargoed

A typically rural scene from yesteryear at the top of Bedwellty Road, Aberbargoed, shows Neuaddwen Farm at the junction where the road divides into two. The old road continues to Bedwellty Church, Pantycefn Road leads to Markham. It became Neuadd Wen, a public house, in the late 1960s.

Bargoed Colliery

Two views of Bargoed Colliery from the top of Puzzle House Hill. The massive tip formed from colliery waste is shown from the opposite direction to that on page 50. The colliery was sunk in 1897, and produced coal from 1901 to 1977. It was the largest colliery in the valley, at one time employing 2,500 men. At its close, the number employed had slumped to 360.

Lower High Street, Bargoed

This photograph shows Lower High Street when its many businesses were thriving. Palace Cinema was on the right. New Hall Cinema, destroyed by a fire in 1958, was opposite. F. W. Woolworth's was built on the New Hall site; this closed comparatively recently when the company went into liquidation. Lower High Street is now a one-way street, from Hanbury Road out of town.

The Pierhead Building, Bargoed

An early picture of the Emporium, also known as the Pierhead Building. The clock, built *c.* 1904, was said to be modelled on the Palace of Westminster's. It was also said to be one of the largest mechanical clocks in South Wales, but has now been removed.

Hanbury Road, Bargoed

This photograph was taken soon after the end of the First World War. The old businesses have disappeared. The street has become one-way, with parking permitted on one side. There is now ample parking behind the properties on the right, but the large number of steps deters many from using it.

Trafalgar Square, Bargoed

Trafalgar Square was originally the site of the town's war memorial, unveiled in 1923. Buses used to put down and pick up their passengers on the three sides of the triangle, but redevelopment means that most of the sheltered bus stops are now within the triangle. The memorial was moved to a site in the park in the 1950s, and was moved yet again to a plot at the rear of St Gwlady's Church in 2002.

41

Aberbargoed from Bargoed

Looking north-east up the valley towards Aberbargoed hill. Bargoed Colliery, which was sunk in 1897, produced coal from 1901 to 1977. It was the largest colliery in the upper part of the valley. A consequence was that Bargoed was a thriving town. Alas, this is not so today. Great effort has been made to improve the road system. The new road on the right of the lower photograph allows service buses a much easier haul between Bargoed and Aberbargoed than when they had to attack the hill.

Commercial Street, Gilfach

A milk float stands on Commercial Street prior to the First World War, on its journey towards Bargoed. Beyond the house on the right is the Presbyterian chapel, which was demolished some years ago. Two of the oriel windows to the left, very fashionable at one time, have been removed.

Commercial Street, Aberbargoed

More than 100 years separate these photographs of the north end of Commercial Street. During the intervening years, a large Duffryn Hotel has been built in the distance. Subsequently, it housed the main offices and council chamber of Bedwellty Urban District Council until their new complex was built between Blackwood and Pontllanfraith. The building is now a block of flats.

The Cottage Hospital, Aberbargoed

Aberbargoed Cottage Hospital was built by John Lloyd of Ystrad Mynach for the Powell Duffryn Steam Coal Company, at a cost of £4,000. Opened in 1909, it had four wards, an operating theatre and living quarters for some of the nursing staff. It is still in use.

Aberbargoed War Memorial

These memorial gates were erected in Commercial Street, Aberbargoed, to commemorate the young men of the village who had given their lives for king and country in the First World War. The new main road from Bargoed, along which the bus service operates (preferring it to the steep Aberbargoed hill), means that this memorial is now far more conspicuous than it used to be.

An Aberbargoed Chemist

The shop front is identical, apart from the colour of the paintwork, but many decades separate these two photographs of the chemist's shop in the centre of Commercial Street, Aberbargoed. Pharmacist P. Hopkinson has replaced Penry S. Thomas.

The Institute, Aberbargoed

The Workmen's Library and Institute, Commercial Street, was built in 1907 with help from the Powell Duffryn Steam Coal Company. This is how it looked prior to the First World War. When it was closed, it was converted into a nursing home; it is now Bridavan Care Home.

Dancing around the Maypole

Young children dance around the maypole in front of what is now St Peter's Church, Aberbargoed. They are watched by local dignitaries. Adjacent to this modern church, built just over fifty years ago, is the new residence of the Rector of Bedwellty, enabling her to be much closer to her flock than when the rectory was near Bedwellty Church. It is a Monday evening, so members of Aberbargoed Ladies' Choir are arriving for practice.

Europe's Largest Spoil Tip
Once said to be the largest coal tip in Europe, this great scar on the landscape has been totally removed. People living in Pengam Road, Aberbargoed, can now see the sun setting over the distant horizon. There was another tip on the opposite side of the road, which stretched almost to the boundary wall of Bedwellty Church.

Britannia Colliery, Pengam

When this photograph was taken, Britannia employed more than 2,000 men. All of the plant was powered by electricity. It had two shafts, one at 1,844 feet and the other at 2,142 feet, and was always considered a very wet mine. Closed in 1983, nature has reclaimed much of the site. A pair of mallards now lives on the site of the former sidings.

Lewis School, Pengam

This grammar school was founded in 1729, but it was 1760 before the first fifteen boys were taught in a house near Gelligaer Church. The school moved to the present site in 1848 and by 1850 this Tudor Gothic building had opened. There was a major rebuild and extension, including a Master's House, in 1902. When it became part of the comprehensive system, new buildings were constructed on the opposite side of the road. The old school was demolished in 2002.

St Catwg's Church, Gelligaer

St Catwg's was heavily restored by Charles Buckeridge in 1867/68 under the influence of Rector Gilbert Harris. A baptismal font allowing baptism by total immersion was installed, possibly to discourage adults from joining the Baptists. While the present building can be traced back to the Norman priests, the foundation is believed to date from the sixth century, when it was one of the churches established by the Celtic saints. From the tower it is possible to see the neighbouring churches of Bedwellty, Mynyddislwyn and Eglwysilan.

Harp Inn, Gelligaer

Standing proudly on the corner opposite the parish church is the large Harp Inn. Close inspection of the photograph shows that the proprietor was Rowland Morgan. There was good stabling, and the pub was tied to the Taff Vale Brewery Company. The Harp was also the local headquarters of the Royal Antediluvian Order of Buffaloes, a fraternal social organisation that supports the British Crown and constitution. It is still a public house.

Ploughing

Nothing has changed more in the valley than the farms. These pictures illustrate a great leap forward in the way land was ploughed. The most recent picture shows P. J. Skyrme on his tractor, pulling a two-furrow plough. He was the World Champion Ploughman and is shown here in a ploughing competition in a field adjacent to Llancaeach Fawr, which has been described as the most perfectly preserved Elizabethan mansion in Glamorgan. The other photograph shows how it used to be done; with a pair of horses ploughing a single furrow at a time.

Commercial Road, Pengam (1)
This is looking in the direction of The Smith's Arms. The old school at the end of the terrace is now Ysgol Guffyn Trelyn, a Welsh medium school. The children transfer to Ysgol Cwm Rhymney, Fleur de Lis, for their secondary education.

Commercial Road, Pengam (II)

These photographs were taken from the junction with St David's Road. The colliery and sidings have disappeared and the land has been reclaimed. A new primary school and some bungalows have been built on part of the site; Mother Nature is doing her best to improve the remainder.

Ebenezer Baptist Church, Pengam
Ebenezer as it looked in 1925 and as it looks today. Much time, effort, and money has been expended on the building recently; this includes a significant extension.

Capel's Corner

An early photograph of one corner of the crossroads at the junction of St David's Road and Pengam Road. This spot has been known for decades as 'Capel's', after one of the first garages in the area. Petrol was served from pumps on the edge of the road, something unthinkable today. Capel's has expanded and moved a little closer to Aberbargoed. The original building is now occupied by C&S Heating and PDQ Electrical.

A River Bridge between Fleur-de-Lis and Pengam

This simple bridge allows pedestrians to cross the Rhymney River. Recently replaced, the crossing still satisfies a need.

Flower Institute

Pengam and Fleur-de-Lis Workmen's Institute and Library, financed by local miners' contributions and a grant from the miners' union, was built in 1911. As the social centre of the village, it was extended between the wars into the three-storey building it is today. There was a large concert hall on the top floor, a snooker hall, library, and reading room on the floor beneath, and a dance hall with a stage on the ground floor.

High Street, Fleur-de-Lis (I)

The properties on this side of the street, seen from the north, are virtually unchanged. The English Congregational Church, now the United Reformed Church, is set back in the gap halfway along. Bungalows for older residents have been built on the opposite side of the street.

High Street, Fleur-de-Lis (II)

Looking towards the 'stute, the Trelyn Hotel has been replaced by houses. The home of the local rugby club – who are, at the time of writing, top of the Welsh National League, Division Three East – is opposite. Their home games are played at Trelyn Park.

High Street, Fleur-de-Lis (III)

The butcher's shop of J. Davies & Sons, owned by the Brooks family and seen here looking south, has closed. Other businesses thrive. Chemist Vida Rogers expanded into the adjacent shop. Salem Welsh Congregational Church (built in 1860) on the left and the Trelyn Hotel on the right have disappeared. Houses have been built in their place.

Trelyn Lane, Fleur-de-Lis

A delivery man with his young assistant pose with their bread cart (which belonged to the local Co-operative Society) halfway down Trelyn Lane. About the only things that link these two pictures are the ornate iron railings.

The Square, Fleur-de-Lis

When this photograph was taken *c.* 1920, this was a busy business area. All the shops have now been converted into houses. Note the gas lamp in the middle of the road. How long would that survive today? Further along was an antiques shop. Gerry Barber's Fleur-de-Lis Antiques is in the same block in 2010.

Fleur-de-Lis Station

Looking north at Fleur-de-Lis station, this prospective passenger is waiting for a train to travel down the valley. All that is common to the two pictures is part of the gable end of a house. Bude Terrace is to the right. The removal of the station buildings reveals Ivor Street to the camera. A bungalow has been built on the platform, with a vegetable garden adjacent.

Trelyn Park, Fleur-de-Lis

Trelyn Park once had a bowling green, a pavilion, and a children's playground. There were also tennis courts and a cricket square. All seem to have vanished, but for every negative there is usually a positive, and now rugby is catered for better than ever. A floodlit surfaced square is available for practice on those cold, wet winter nights when it would be unwise to use the field.

Bryn Meadows Golf and Country Club

This is Bedwas Uchaf Farm, just north of Maesycwmmer, as it was when it was bought in 1972 by Edgar Jeffries, Dave Belton, Brian Hinks, and Brian Mayo, four enthusiastic golfers. Under the Mayo family, it has become Bryn Meadows Golf and Country Club, a prestigious eighteen-hole golf course with an imposing forty-two-room hotel, a club house, a health spa with swimming pool, and a self-contained function room. As the modern photograph shows, the old house was incorporated into the complex.

King's Hill, Hengoed

This is the part of King's Hill, below the Cardiff-Rhymney railway line. Formerly two-storey houses, they were converted into three-storey buildings with shops at ground level. Progress has determined that the shops have closed and the properties have become flats. The Junction Hotel, now hidden by the taller buildings, remains well patronised.

Brynavon Terrace, Hengoed

When this photograph was taken in Brynavon, almost all household needs could be purchased from the local shops. Interestingly, all four oriel windows, which were a common feature over shop fronts for properties of the period, remain intact.

Gelligaer Council Offices, Hengoed

This building, dating from 1897 and situated at one end of Park Road, was the home of Gelligaer and Rhigos Rural District Council. By 1908, the new Gelligaer UDC was administered from it. In spite of the old fire station being at road level in front of this highly ornate Victorian building, the offices were destroyed by fire in 1968. Living accommodation now occupies the site.

Park Road, Hengoed

A century ago, these large houses were the most desirable properties in the area, being close to the stations on two railway lines and with good views over the valley to the south and east. An annoyance to some of the residents was the goods train that thundered along the line in front of them at 1 a.m.

Hengoed Girls' County School (I)

High up on King's Hill, Hengoed, an intermediate school for girls was opened on 1 November 1900, as shown in this poor quality image. It would be known as Hengoed Girls' County School, its origin dating back to the will of Edward Lewis in 1729. Due to colliery workings, the ground on which it stood became unstable. A new school was officially opened on 17 May 1960 at Oakfield Street, Ystrad Mynach. Merging with the local secondary school, it became Lewis Girls' Comprehensive School in 1973.

Hengoed Girls' County School (II)

The all-female staff of Hengoed Girls' County School, with the head girl, in 1948. The headmistress is Miss G. M. Richards. Sitting to her right is Miss Ethel Moore, who would follow Miss Richards as head. It is now much larger, with boys attending some of the A-level courses and has a truly mixed staff. The headmistress shown below is Dr Sue Noake; next to her is Deputy Head Mrs Catherine Rogerson, who would later become headmistress.

Hengoed viaduct

This viaduct is a magnificent stone structure 850 feet long. It was designed by Charles Liddell in 1857, and was built on a curve, to carry trains across the Rhymney Valley. It has sixteen arches that carried a double track of the railway linking Pontypool with Neath, and was last used for passenger traffic in 1964. These pictures are taken looking from Hengoed towards Maesycwmmer. Cyclists and pedestrians are the only traffic now.

Maesycwmmer Railway Station

The station at Maesycwmmer is on the Brecon and Merthyr line connecting Brecon and Newport. Both photographs are taken from the same spot. The Butchers Arms, the further public house, has closed, but The Angel is very much in business. Passing under the partially hidden arch is the ancient road to Fleur-de-Lis.

Maesycwmmer Butcher's

The building on the right was originally a greengrocer's and a general store. Later, it was occupied by Evan Woodward, a butcher. Woodward was succeeded by Brian Crane, who is still in business. Several properties on the opposite side of the road have been demolished to widen the road. The Maesycwmmer Inn stands on the right. Access for pedestrians to the viaduct is from a path up the slope to the left.

Commercial Road, Maesycwmmer

Prior to the Second World War, this was the main road through the village. But as a result of major roadworks in the 1960s, the road has become a quiet side road running parallel to the new road. It is comparatively easy to park for a short time and visit these shops.

Glen View, Maesycwmmer

A scene that is almost as quiet today as when the first picture was taken in the 1960s. Sheltered housing, known as Y Glyn, is on the right at the end of the street.

Maesycwmmer Open-air Swimming Pool

Our climate is hardly suitable for an open-air swimming pool, but there was great enthusiasm for such things in the 1930s. Maesycwmmer's pool was built by the local Welfare Association on land donated by Miss Richards of Gwernau Farm. Many locals helped in its construction, either by raising money, by supplying labour, or simply by serving refreshments to the workers. Inevitably, the pool closed, replaced by an indoor pool in a nearby town. The Community Centre now stands on the site.

Penallta Colliery

Although the colliery closed in 1991, the large engine hall, some 300-feet long and seventy-feet wide, together with headgear for the two shafts, is still intact. This hall has sixteen bays separated by red brick columns. This was the last working colliery in the Rhymney Valley. Sinking began in 1906, and the first coal was mined three years later. By the mid 1930s, the labour force had risen to more than 3,000, but after the Second World War there was a slow but steady decline.

Bedwlwyn Road, Ystrad Mynach (I)

How this scene has changed! Even the beech tree is different. When the old tree was found to be rotten, it was removed and two young trees were planted in the hope that one of them would take root. The modern picture shows that one of them has indeed become a substantial tree. The Beech Tree Hotel is on the right. Immediately ahead, at the other side of the roundabout, is the business of D. Emlyn Lloyd.

Bedwlwyn Road, Ystrad Mynach (II)
This scene is from before the 1920s. The road has not been surfaced and the pavement is incomplete. A gas lamp on the corner is the only evidence of street lighting. One of the shops belongs to the Bracchi family. Their café was once the social mecca of the village.

Penallta Road, Ystrad Mynach

This is the west side of the road, looking north from the Pierhead building. Just two shops are visible in this photograph, taken a century ago. Between then and now, many businesses have opened and closed.

The Pierhead Site, Ystrad Mynach

Thought to have been taken about 100 years ago, this photograph of Bedwlwyn Road was taken before the Pierhead Building was erected in 1912. The cottage on the left was known as Pontargylla. The Pierhead Building, which has a lot of architectural similarities with the one in Bargoed, became the village's prime shopping area. This block looked out on The Square and was probably the reason many shops opened on Penallta Road and Bedwlwyn Road. In recent years, many of the village's shops have closed.

Commercial Street, Ystrad Mynach (I)

People gather in The Square to the left of the radio business belonging to E. Gethin Morgan and John Abbiss. It is 1936, and they have been listening to Edward VIII's abdication speech. Even the village bobby has arrived – he rests his bicycle against the telegraph post. A farmer walks towards the camera; behind him is a mother carrying a baby wrapped in 'Welsh fashion'. In the same building today, radios have been replaced by that most basic of needs, fish and chips.

Commercial Street Ystrad Mynach (II)
The pony and trap stand outside a gents' outfitters. Always selling gents' clothing, by the 1960s it was known as The Bon and was owned by John Perkins, a Blackwood nonagenarian who liked to walk everywhere. Subsequently, Lyn Tudor was in business here. At present it is Dyfed Menswear, specialising in formal wear for weddings and other important occasions.

The Royal Oak Hotel, Ystrad Mynach

It is difficult to believe, but these two photographs, taken near Ystrad Mynach Bridge, show the same site with two totally different public houses, both named the Royal Oak. More than a century separates them. The old building gave way to the new one, which dominates the road junction, just prior to the First World War.

Tredomen

The photographs on these facing pages show the former site of Powell Duffryn's engineering works after it was cleared for redevelopment. Built in 1922 to make and supply mining equipment for their many collieries, it was taken over by the National Coal Board in 1950, and then contracted out as the coal industry was run down. The rectangular building in the distance became the NCB

computer centre, but it is now the home of Caerphilly County Borough Museums and Heritage. In the background is the village of Tredomen. The modern photographs show the area as Tredomen Business Park. The circular building on the left is a conference centre, other buildings bring together local business support agencies and training facilities organised by The College, Ystrad Mynach. Just out of shot to the right is Ty Penallta, the administrative offices of Caerphilly Borough Council.

Ystrad Mynach Bridge

The bridge that crosses the Rhymney River at Ystrad Mynach allows the road from Maesycwmmer to link with the main road from the village to Caerphilly. Built soon after the end of the Second World War, it was wide for the time – there was, after all, little traffic. The old school was to the right and the Cottage Dance Centre is just over the bridge to the left.

Rhymney Valley Hospital

Ystrad Fawr was the home of the Lindsay family. Colonel Henry Morgan Lindsay was a soldier, politician, and renowned sportsman. He became Deputy Lieutenant for Glamorgan, a member of the governing body of the Welsh Church, and a Knight of the Order of St John. Subsequent to the family leaving the property, it became the council's offices. When the council moved to palatial new premises at Tredomen, the site was cleared and a modern General Hospital built on it.

Coopers Arms, Ystrad Mynach

Coopers Arms is opposite the new hospital on the old road from the village to Llanbradach. In the early years, they brewed their own beer here and were licensed to open very early in the morning to serve miners when they came off the night shift. An interesting historical fact is that when Katherine, the daughter of Reverend George Thomas of Ystrad Fawr, got married in October 1858, 200 members of the tenantry sat down here for a substantial dinner. One wonders where they all sat.

Ystrad Mynach Mill

Not a scene one would expect to see in an industrial valley that relied so much on iron and coal. This is the mill and forge on the old road from Ystrad Mynach to Caerphilly, just below Coopers Arms. A forge operated here for more than four centuries and the first post office in the area was in this house. The house has been significantly upgraded.

Howard Jones, Pontlottyn

Howard Jones, one of the few remaining businesses on The Square, is also one of the most fascinating shops in the valley. There is even a small museum upstairs. Should you want keys cut, plants or compost for the garden, pet foods, gas, hardware, ironmongery, or even mothballs to protect your clothes or blacklead for your old grate, you can get it here.

Acknowledgements

Very many people have helped with the production of this book by making useful suggestions and furnishing me with information and old photographs. I am most grateful to Gerry Barber, Mike Carey, Malcolm Davies, Peter Downing, Graham James, Molly Jenkins, Jill Jones, Howard Jones, Huw Jones, Joyce Jones, Tony Leach, Fay Mayo, Gethin Morgan, the late Reg Nash, Ron Owens, Derek and Audrey Packer, John Price, Delyth Robinson, Islwyn Richards, Caryl Thomas, Hetty Watkins, and Edward Williams-Price. In particular, I would like to thank my wife Betty and my good friend John Watkins for reading the whole book and making many useful observations.